NOTEWORTHY PARENTING
ROADMAP

A Companion JOURNAL to Note Your Best PARENTING IDEAS

KRISTIN BUCHTEL

Noteworthy Parenting Roadmap: A Companion Journal to Note Your Best Parenting IDEAS
Published by Booktell Press
Denver, CO

ISBN: 978-1-7340843-1-3

SELF-HELP / Journaling

Cover and Interior design by Victoria Wolf

QUANTITY PURCHASES: Schools, companies, professional groups, clubs, and other organizations may qualify for special terms when ordering quantities of this title. For information, email Kristin@noteworthyparenting.com.

Use this journal as a companion to

Noteworthy Parenting:
How to Use Your Own IDEAS to Create Your Parenting Roadmap

Available on Amazon or
at NoteworthyParenting.com

INTRODUCTION

"If you fail to plan, you are planning to fail."
— Benjamin Franklin

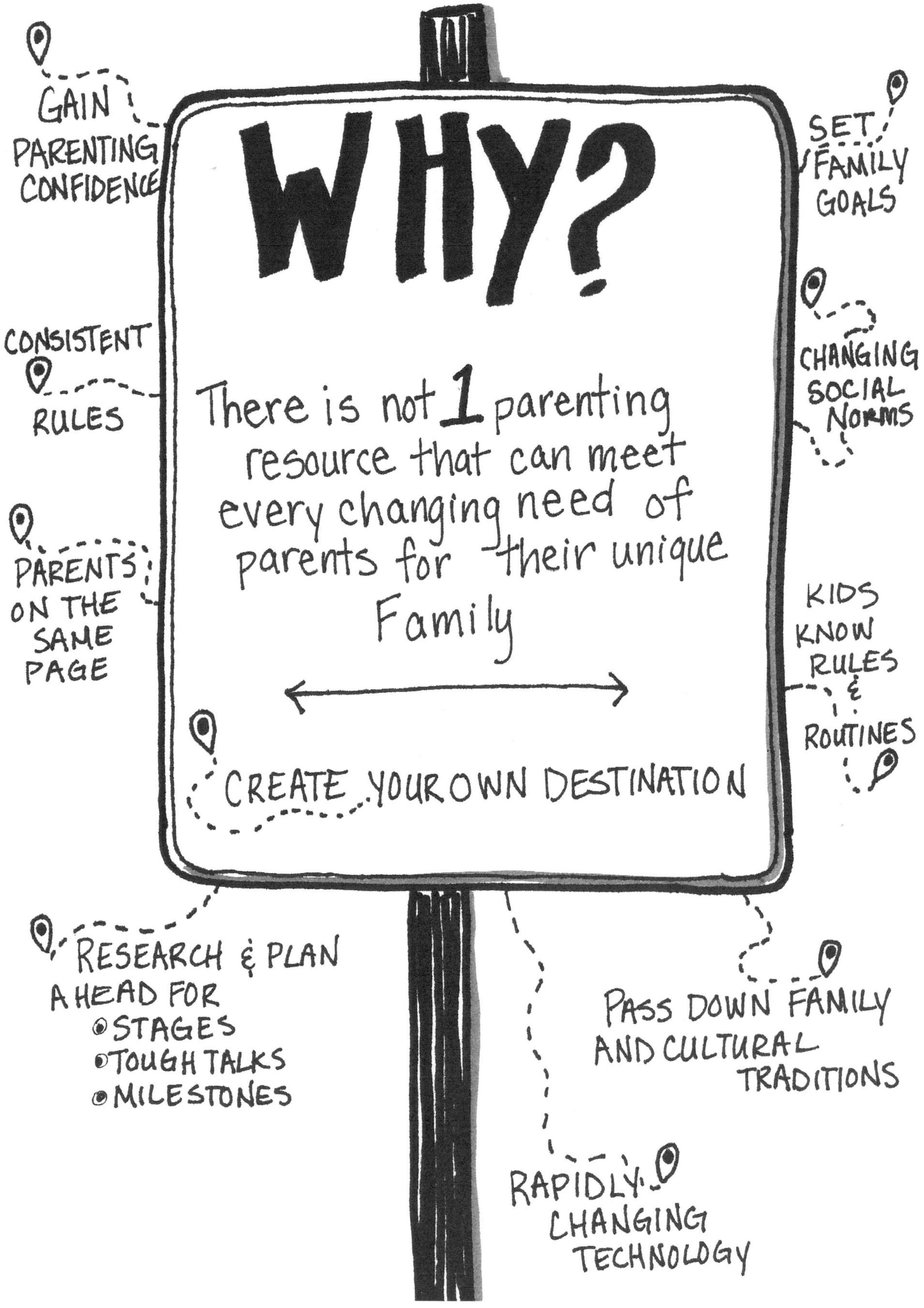
WHY?
There is not 1 parenting resource that can meet every changing need of parents for their unique Family
CREATE YOUR OWN DESTINATION
GAIN PARENTING CONFIDENCE
SET FAMILY GOALS
CONSISTENT RULES
CHANGING SOCIAL NORMS
PARENTS ON THE SAME PAGE
KIDS KNOW RULES & ROUTINES
RESEARCH & PLAN AHEAD FOR
• STAGES
• TOUGH TALKS
• MILESTONES
PASS DOWN FAMILY AND CULTURAL TRADITIONS
RAPIDLY CHANGING TECHNOLOGY

The saying goes that *there is no instruction manual for raising kids*, but I would like to think that the companion book *Noteworthy Parenting*, along with this Parenting Roadmap, is a step in the right direction.

No two human beings are the same—no two parents and no two kids. Your family is unique; therefore, your parenting will be unique.

Likewise, there are no single plans, tips, or classes that will have every perfect answer for your parenting. You must choose the advice that works for you. Tweak the tips and hacks to fit your needs. Make your own parenting path!

As a parent or parenting team, discuss and write down the ideas, tips, goals, and advice that you want to use and remember on the journey of raising your kids. You are the author(s) of this Parenting Roadmap.

Prioritizing your roadmap will empower your parenting, reduce regrets, enhance confidence, and encourage consistency and focus in your parenting.

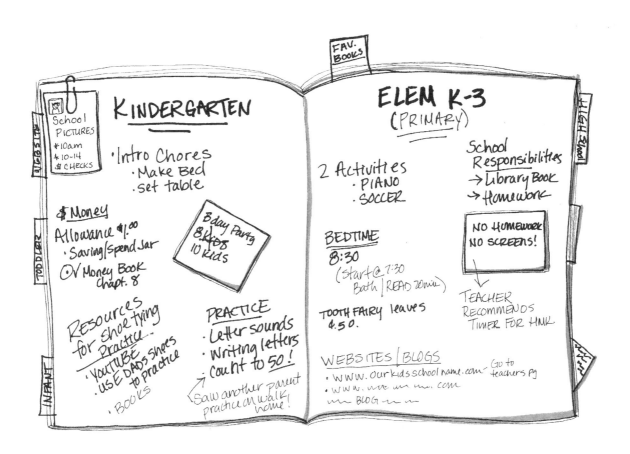

HOW TO USE THIS JOURNAL

This journal is not intended to be a literary masterpiece or an artfully designed scrapbook, but simply a gathering space for your parenting plan.

The feel of your Parenting Roadmap is similar to that of an old family recipe book. There may be recipe cards taped into the book, or handwritten adjustments for special ingredients. Some pages are bent or bookmarked. Printed articles might be stuffed into the appropriate section. It may not look pretty, but the notes and information inside are valuable and useful for you and maybe the next generation to refer to.

Any notetaking style will do; just keep it quick, useful, and handy. If you find a great tidbit to add to your Parenting Roadmap, but you do not have it handy, text it to yourself, screenshot it, grab a piece of paper and jot yourself a note. Then make sure it gets put into the right section of your roadmap! Even if it means printing that text to yourself and taping it into your roadmap.

Do you need to update or tweak a part of the plan? Are you ready to plan for upcoming stages? Are you tracking your progress toward attaining your family goals?

Add the maintenance of your Parenting Road-map to your calendar, in order to keep your road-map useful and current. Set aside time to monitor your plan's effectiveness by adding date nights or special times to review your plans.

ROADMAP PAGES

The main part of the Parenting Roadmap is set up by the following ages:

- Infant
- Toddler
- Preschool
- Primary Grades (K-2)
- Secondary Grades (3-5)
- Middle School
- High School
- Young Adult

HERE ARE SOME SAMPLE PAGES:

PRESCHOOL

- SIGNED UP FOR AM (T/TH) PRESCHOOL 8:30-11.
  - SaVe FAVORITE PAPERS IN SCHOOL BIN
  - SCHOOL PICTURES
    - ✱Grandmas→5x7's
  - OK TO BRING COOKIES TO CLASS ON BDAY

SHARING STRUGGLES <u>PLAN</u>
- Get BOOKS on Sharing from Library
- PRACTICE ACTING OUT SHARING
- Consequences - loss of toy hot shared for 1-2 days.

FAMILY ACTIVITIES
↓
<u>GOALS</u>
- Weekly library
- PARK/PICNICS
- PUMPKIN PATCH
- TOY DRIVE

<u>BEDTIME</u>
8:00
(START 7:30)
- Jamies
- 2 STORIES
- BRUSH TEETH
- POTTY

<u>STRANGERS</u>
✓ OUT Berenstain Bears Learn About Strangers

Starting to give up naps! ☺
- Quiet time
- Read BOOKS
- Puzzles
- Set a timer

THINGS TO PRACTICE

- LETTER SOUNDS
- PEDDLING A BIKE
- SWIMMING Lessons
- Sharing

GOOD IDEAS YOU TUBE

REC CTR - summer 2 week sessions

CHORES

① PICK UP TOYS
② HANG UP COAT
③ PUT DIRTY CLOTHES IN BASKET

✓ OUT NOTEWORTHY PARENTING.COM
- BLOG

HIGH SCHOOL

BUDGET
- SCHOOL FEES
  PROM / SEN. PICTS
  YEARBOOK
  Testing Fees
  Sports fees
  Art fees
  parking pass
  fundraisers
  musical costumes/props
    instruments
  UNIFORMS

Driving
- Permit
- Driving School
  - Take driving test there
- Laws / RULES
  Review @ Permit @ License
- √ with Auto Insurance

FAMILY TIME / Meetups
- SAT. MORN BREAKFAST
- MOVIES (AVENGERS!)
  - Weekend trip to Mountains Sept.
- FIRE PIT

THE SYSTEM
· CREATED TOGETHER ·
- CURFEW 11:30
- Plug electronics in parents room to charge by 10:00 PM
- PARENTS' √ Grades every 2 weeks
- Kids pay gas + entertainment
- PARENTS PAY for PROM RIDE, Clothes.
  75⁰⁰ for clothes
- KIDS PAY FOR PROM TICKETS / DINNER
- CHORES DONE BY SAT @ 5 PM

Mom Dad
Kid Kids

GIVE A HEADS UP
AT 18
- PAY CAR INSURANCE
- CAR OIL CHANGES
- FULL TIME STUDENT OR RENT
- √ in on $ matters

JOB
10-20 hours WEEK

MATH TUTOR
NEEDED FOR
MOM! ☺
LOL!

GRAD PARTY DETAILS
UNDER SPECIAL Events!

6

I have added pages in the back to help with other aspects of your parenting journey:

FAMILY GOALS

Write down the goals you have as a family and break them down into smaller pieces or keep a schedule, so you stay on track toward achieving your goals! Maybe you want to take the kids to Europe, or run a 10K charity race.

PARENT PAGES

Keep track of babysitters, your adult goals, and lists of how you would like to spend your "kid free" time.

TRADITIONS, CUSTOMS, AND HOLIDAYS

To keep notes of who is hosting Thanksgiving dinner this year, or a list of Santa's gift-giving parameters, and maybe a note about how much the Tooth Fairy leaves for a tooth.

SPECIAL EVENTS

Details for birthdays, graduations, and weddings. This helps when younger siblings come along so you can remember how much you spent and the general outline of events.

GIFTS GIVEN

A great sheet to keep track of how much you spent for holidays, birthdays, graduations, and weddings not only for your kids, but for nieces, nephews, and friends. This is helpful a few years later when a younger sibling graduates or gets married and you can't remember what gift you gave a few years back.

CONTRACTS

Keep track of loans you give your kids for extras, or for checking grades, or any agreement that you feel requires more accountability. You add the stipulations, dates and details, and all parties sign and date it.

7

BLANK

Provided for any extra topics that you would like to add to your Parenting Roadmap.

HERE ARE A FEW SAMPLE PAGES:

SPECIAL EVENTS

WHO is the Event For?	WHAT is the Occasion?	DETAILS
ALL OF OUR KIDS	Elementary Birthday Parties	• INVITE 8 KIDS *SATURDAY NEAR BDAY • PIZZA • STORE DECORATED CAKE
HUBBY'S PARENTS	25TH ANNIV. PARTY	• NOTES UNDER FAMILY FILE WE DID: DECORATIONS, CAKE AND INVITES
Ashley's Graduation 2010	Graduation High School Party	Catered BBQ - 75 people Cake rented tables and chairs for back yard. Details attached.
ALL OF OUR KIDS	WEDDINGS	• BUDGET 20,000 - includes our gift • THEY CHOOSE VENUE/PLANS • INCLUDES RENTAL OF CLOTHES FOR SIBS. DETAILS under Young Adult section.

GIFTS GIVEN

WHO is the Gift For?	WHAT is the occasion?	DATE	DETAILS
Jake	16th B.day	3/25/10	• $ TOWARDS letter Jacket He pays Remainder 50⁰⁰
SALLY (FRIEND OF daughter FAMILY)	**WEDDING**	6/30/16	• Wine glasses • Wine opener • cheese plate/knife 100⁰⁰
ALL FAMILY	HIGH SCHOOL GRADUATION	—	100.00 CHECK
FRIENDS KIDS	HIGH SCHOOL GRADUATION	—	50⁰⁰ CHECK
MY PARENTS	CHRISTMAS		• DONATE TO CHARITY INSTEAD OF GIFTS. $/100⁰⁰

Contract

SUBJECT: HOMEWORK EXPECTATIONS? LOANS? MOVING BACK IN? CHORES?

DATES CONTRACT IS IN EFFECT: _____

DETAILS:
- WHAT ARE PARENTS RESPONSIBLE FOR?
- WHAT ARE KID(S) RESPONSIBLE FOR?
- HOW WILL LOANS BE PAID BACK?
- ARE THERE CONSEQUENCES? REWARDS?
- USE THIS TO GET ON THE SAME PAGE WITH KID(S).
- TERMS CAN BE DECIDED AS PARENTS OR AS A FAMILY.

SIGN AND DATE:

PARENTS: _Mom_   _Dad_ _____

KID(S): _Kids   Kids   Kids   Kids_ _____

_____

Parenting is not about being pretty and it's not about being perfect.
It's about the power in your parenting plan...

THINK IT... NOTE IT... PARENT IT.

BEGIN!!

INFANT

TODDLER

PRESCHOOL

PRIMARY GRADES (K-2)

SECONDARY GRADES (3-5)

MIDDLE SCHOOL

HIGH SCHOOL

YOUNG ADULT

FAMILY GOALS

TRADITIONS, CUSTOMS, AND HOLIDAYS

SPECIAL EVENTS

WHO is the Event For?	WHAT is the Occasion?	DETAILS

WHO is the Event For?	WHAT is the Occasion?	DETAILS

WHO is the Event For?	WHAT is the Occasion?	DETAILS

WHO is the Event For?	WHAT is the Occasion?	DETAILS

GIFTS GIVEN

WHO is the Gift For?	WHAT is the Occasion?	DATE	DETAILS

WHO is the Gift For?	WHAT is the Occasion?	DATE	DETAILS

WHO is the Gift For?	WHAT is the Occasion?	DATE	DETAILS

WHO is the Gift For?	WHAT is the Occasion?	DATE	DETAILS

CONTRACTS

Contract

Subject:_____

Dates contract is in effect:_____

Details:

Sign and Date:

Parents:_____

Kid(s):_____

_____

Contract

SUBJECT: _____

DATES CONTRACT IS IN EFFECT: _____

DETAILS:

SIGN AND DATE:

PARENTS: _____

KID(S): _____

_____

Contract

SUBJECT: _____

DATES CONTRACT IS IN EFFECT: _____

DETAILS:

SIGN AND DATE:

PARENTS: _____

KID(S): _____

_____

Contract

SUBJECT: _____

DATES CONTRACT IS IN EFFECT: _____

DETAILS:

SIGN AND DATE:

PARENTS: _____

_____

KID(S): _____

_____

PARENT PAGES

NOTES